HOW WE SLEEP AT NIGHT

A Mother's Memoir By:

Sara Cunningham

ISBN: 1499725388
ISBN-13: 978-1499725384

Dedicated to:
Parker Trent. My brave dancing boy.

Special thanks to:
My family. I don't deserve them.
Jason and Holli Burnfield. They ran with me.
Glimmers of Hope. May we all be one.

CONTENTS

INTRODUCTION

Homosexuality and religion are not topics I would have chosen for my first book. First of all, my idea of producing a book was to have it *made*, as in the kind you make at Copy Fast or Walgreens, better known as a book-*let*. I imagined my first booklet to be titled 'My Jeep Book' a small and simple book, suitable for a coffee table, full of interesting Jeep photos I've collected over the years. But noooo, instead I have been consumed with producing 'How We Sleep At Night' a book that required my soul and a ISBN number. The title was conceived one sleepless night (out of a thousand) when I laid in my bed, sick with worry about the salvation of my gay son. The contents were labored over and over and over again until finally "How we Sleep at Night" was birthed out of love, respect and obligation to Parker Trent, the church and the gay community. 'My Jeep Book' can wait. And so we begin.

Many details in this book are from personal conversations and situations that span from the beginning of Parker 'coming out', dating and then getting married to his partner Kohl. Some of these moments are healing, painful and ongoing, for that reason I chose to be vague with some of the details that might identify specific people or places. It is not my intention to point out, glorify or disrespect any one person, religion, or place of business. Explicit language is used for lack of a better word.

Unless noted otherwise, Parker created all of the art used in this book, the cover is reminiscent of the night sky painted on his bedroom ceiling for 21 years, the beds and people sleeping were made from 'Thank You' notes that he and Kohl sent after their wedding. Parker wrote and recorded most of the songs at home when he was young, some are rough but the sentiment is there. Hope you'll take a listen using the links provided at the end of each song.

IF I DIDN'T WANT TO KNOW

If I didn't want to know - what you're thinkin' when you're
sleepin'
Then I wouldn't close my eyes like our parents taught us to
If I didn't want to know - where your heart goes when you're
dreamin'
Then I wouldn't rest my head on this pillow next to you
If I didn't want to know- if you'll be here when the sun is
Then I wouldn't stick around – then I wouldn't follow through

Words & music by Parker Cunningham

http://www.theburnfieldcastle.com/01_if_i_didnt_want_to_know.m4a

CHAPTER ONE
IN THE BEGINNING

~Two little love birds sittin' in a tree k.i.s.s.i.n.g~

~first comes baby then comes marriage~

Wait…what?

I remember the first time I thought about Rex as *more* than a friend. His sister Sue and I were best friends and their family invited me to join them for dinner at the A&A café. It was a little restaurant located in the neighborhood where we lived. This was the kind of diner that served homemade french fries, fruit pies and each table had a mini juke box that included one of my personal favorites, Captain and Tennille's *Love will keep us together.*

I sat across from him in the corner booth and that was the first time *(Love, love will keep us together, think of me babe whenever some sweet talking girl comes along singing her song)* I noticed his big brown eyes, the tone of his skin, *(Don't mess around, you gotta be strong-just stop (stop) 'cause I really love you)* his hands and his perfectly feathered hair. *(Stop (stop), I'll be thinking of you. Look in my heart and let love keep us togeeetherrr ~ what ever ~wa wa wa what ever!)* Oh my.

It would be three years later, one hot summer and a two-piece bathing suit before Rex even knew I existed.

We dated off and on, he got his own apartment and I got pregnant. It was horrible timing. I mean, Rex and I really liked each other, (duh) but we weren't ready to be married and certainly not ready for children. He was just now living on his own, making his own decisions, going to college and working full time figuring out what he wanted to do with his life.

Me? I hardly had a pot to piss in. My family had recently moved to Colorado and I was living in Oklahoma with a friend and her family while working as a waitress. I was afraid to tell Rex. I was afraid of what his family would think of me. I knew this mistake would ruin any future we had as individuals or as a couple. I blamed myself for not being more careful. I felt so stupid. In one day I became one of *those* girls. Shit! I wanted to hide in a hole and die. I called my mom. She said, "Come on home," and so I ran to Colorado and lived with her there.

For nine months I felt ashamed and guilty for ruining our lives with this unplanned pregnancy, nine months of justifying myself for not telling Rex. I avoided his calls when I could. When we did talk I was vague and did my best to convince him that I wanted to be here and not there, sparing him from what I thought would be certain ruin. (dramatic pause.)

I spent nine months convincing myself that I

could stay in Colorado and raise Travis on my own, no big deal. Nine months of wasted energy vanished the moment Travis was born. He was perfect and I loved him. Suddenly my life had new meaning and direction. Suddenly I had two reasons not to keep this secret from Rex.

#1. Travis was wonderful. How could I keep him a secret?

#2. My mom threatened to call Rex if I didn't.

Rex immediately came to Colorado. We spent time going over the harsh reality of the situation. He respectfully gave me the choice to stay in Colorado or to go back to Oklahoma with him and at least try to make things work. Honestly, I had to think about it. I didn't want to leave the security of my mother and my family. They had already given me so much and were willing to help me with Travis. I had made plans and could see myself living in Colorado but I also knew that I wanted the best for Travis and being a single parent could suck for both of us. Besides, Rex was a great guy. He worked hard and obviously had good values. I mean, he was here wasn't he? And did I mention his chest, arms and legs? ....Oh my! So we packed up and moved to Oklahoma!

We had our share of struggles. Being a young couple adjusting to each other and a new baby all at once was hard. Even though Rex's family welcomed me and adored Travis, we spent a lot of time in survival mode.

When Travis was nine months old we went to the Justice of the Peace and got married. Travis, Sue and my mother were witnesses. Then when Travis was two we bought our house and were working together for the kind of life that we wanted. Life got easier and four years later we (sort of) planned Parker. We went to all the prenatal classes and decorated the nursery. It was a wonderful experience. Parker was born. He was beautiful and we loved him.

The physical similarities between the boys were that they both had brown hair and a penis. Everything else was different. Travis has brown eyes. Parker's are blue. Travis was growing up lean and active, studied well in school and was an all-around American boy. Parker was chubby and less active, daydreamed in school and chose few friends. The four-year age gap proved less of a challenge than the difference in personalities. I rarely had to keep Parker out of Travis' things and vice-versa because their interests were so different. It was very apparent that Travis liked "boy" things and Parker gravitated toward "girl" things.

Parker loved dress up and anything with glitter, he spent time on his hair and cared about his clothes. He was sensitive and more imaginative whereas Travis would sleep in his clothes and then wear them every day if we let him. He didn't *always* use soap, and he was more of a literal thinker. At Halloween, Parker wanted to be Tweety Bird and Travis Batman. Travis watched Ghost Busters and Ninja Turtles, while Parker preferred Fantasia or My Little Pony. You get the idea?

I never thought too much about the differences between the kids when they were little. They were just being themselves and everything seemed normal according to their personalities.

The first time I remember thinking, "that's odd" about Parker's behavior was when he was about five-years-old. We had company at the house and we adults were in the kitchen visiting while Parker and their daughter were upstairs playing. Soon the two came running downstairs and Parker burst into the kitchen wearing a pair of my heels and my flowery flowing dress. He was laughing and dancing and twirling about in the center of the kitchen. All of us were laughing because it was funny, but at the same time we were shocked to see how thrilled he was at that very moment. We had never seen or heard Parker so excited. His laugh was more like a shrill squeal and he danced in that dress until his hair was wet with sweat. It was crazy.

The next morning I was picking up around the house and for some reason the boys and I ended up in Parker's room. Travis made a face of disapproval when he saw the dress and heels strewn on the floor. It was the first time I remember hearing Travis tease Parker about being a girl. It was the first time I remember Travis being annoyed with me for letting Parker play with girl things. It was the first time I felt awkward and torn between my two boys. It was the first time I saw a tension between them that went beyond sibling rivalry.

I found myself making conscious efforts to sway Parker's behavior towards more masculine type things. We spent a lot of time compromising when it came to shopping for toys and clothes. Eventually, Parker would settle for what was picked for him, not that Parker wanted to buy dolls and dresses, (ok well sometimes he wanted to buy dolls) he never seemed content. It was as if he was constantly trying to get comfortable or satisfied with something he didn't want but none of us knew what to give to him or do for him.

Parker enjoyed just being in his room or, if the weather was nice, you'd find him in the back yard perfectly content to be alone. I don't ever recall him complaining about not having a playmate. He could spend hours in the back yard building tiny stick houses in the grass, standing at the fence singing or conversing with himself and watching the cars go by. If the pool was up he was in it, wearing just his underwear, floating for hours on his back, gazing at the sky or swimming face down while tooling around at the bottom. He was always in his head a million miles away. Travis was more outgoing. He had several friends in the neighborhood and they were always running in and out of that front door. If he had some down time he'd play video games or oh, I don't know, teach himself how to ride the unicycle or make a didgeridoo.

Both boys were, and still are extremely creative. They continue to amaze me with their artistic vision and skills.

When they were older and starting school, they participated in afterschool activities. Travis was quick to join Boy Scouts and the baseball team. I made Parker join Cub Scouts. He tried it but after one camping trip, and a couple of den meetings he was over it. He took piano lessons for a while and then later found his niche when he joined and traveled with a successful city children's choir. Rex and I volunteered at the school and were involved in the neighborhood association for several years. We were proud parents. We enjoyed raising our kids and seeing them grow into young adults, respectful towards people, nature and things…*kum~bay~yaaa my looord~*

A few years later Travis was invited to church camp and soon after that we were all going to church. Crestwood Baptist Church, *'a church where you fit in'* the street sign read. The huge blonde brick building was the perfect hub for the neighborhood. A polling place during city and state elections, the neighborhood association met there and during severe weather the basement served as a tornado shelter. I never thought much about the denomination. I just considered myself a Christian who just happened to be plugged into a Baptist church. It made perfect sense to me that we go to a church in our neighborhood and serve the community around it. The small congregation became our church family and the building would be our church home for the better part of 20 years.

If the church doors were open, we were there. We spent summers at Falls Creek, Young Musician's Camp and VBS. When we were in-between or without a youth pastor, a few parents along with myself, would entertain and teach the students what we knew. The church had a couple of fifteen-passenger vans and we were always looking for ways to drive em' around town, to the lake, inner city scavenger hunts, or local peach farms and corn mazes. The youth group had its core students, the ones that came with their parents. Every now and then they would bring a friend or a random kid from the neighborhood would wander in. I enjoyed spending time with all of them.

Being part of this huge church located in the center of the city was like a giant melting pot of society. We saw all sorts of people pass through those front doors, young and old, some were beautiful, some...not so much. The congregation included families with second and third generations sprinkled with blue haired saints. You know, the ones that would shame you for wearing a hat in the 'house of God' and then invite you to go fishing or those that taught Sunday school and smelled like creamed corn. They were for sure, some of my favorite people. We laughed and cried together, played and worked together. We did good things inside and outside of the church. We spent time in each other's homes and our children grew up together. We mourned and celebrated together. Travis and I went with a group to Mexico, Parker and I to India. We took trips of a lifetime with people we loved. We had a *history* together. If one person saw a need that exceeded what they alone could do, the group would work out the details to get it done without hesitation or need of explanation. We served. We prayed. We moved mountains.

CHAPTER TWO
JUST GET THROUGH SCHOOL!

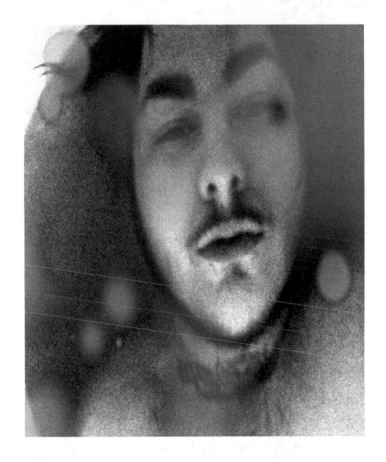

"I thought about it every night, until I fell asleep."

When Parker was ten he said, "Mom, I think I'm gay."

I immediately asked, "Why would you think such a thing?"

He went on to explain that some kids at school teased him on the playground for always playing with the girls and that he acted like a girl.

I cut him off midsentence and sympathized with him, agreeing that kids could be cruel and then encouraged him to stay around his friends. He came back with, "no mom, you don't understand...*I* think *I'm* gay."

I looked intently at him and said, "Why would *you* think such a thing?"

He replied, "I don't *think* like other boys do."

Again, I interrupted and tried to diffuse the conversation by saying that "*these feelings*" were normal hormonal growing pains. It was nothing to dwell on and his job was to focus on school. He agreed, slightly grasping the fact that I did indeed cut him short. We, namely me, talked about other menial things. I awkwardly dismissed him and he went on to his room.

Shit.

It was not our first time to have this type of conversation. I knew Parker was going through *something* but I didn't want to take it too seriously. I refused to entertain the idea that he even *might* be gay. Even the conversations that Rex and I had about it were brief, as I was confident that Parker would outgrow these feelings and I was trusting God to work it all out. I simply was not having it. Rex had a better grip of the situation than I ever did. He has cousins who are gay, and his younger brother Robert was gay. Robert and I went to elementary and middle school together and he was always getting picked on but I thought it was because he was goofy. He survived high school only to get caught up in drugs and alcohol that would plague his adulthood. He would float in and out of our lives and we never knew what to expect when he came for a visit. He always had a new (used) fancy car and jewelry to show off. Robert was the first gay person that the boys and I ever knew. We had moments when he acted like a "normal" uncle but for the rest of his life it was like he was swinging from the chandeliers so to speak. He was loud, flamboyant and full of drama. To us, this was what 'being gay' looked like. Robert was in and out of abusive relationships until he met Terry. They lived together in a small apartment and Terry stayed when others would have left. Robert was in his thirties when he started getting sick. I don't know if it was officially confirmed to the family, but Rex and I believe it was due to complications of the AIDS virus. I remember Rex spending time with Robert, taking groceries or picking up medicine. The time was bitter sweet. It took this horrible illness to settle Robert down and it was Terry that cared for him until he died. I believe it was through the life and loss of Robert that Rex found a way to be sensitive to me while quietly supportive of Parker.

Elementary and Middle school had its challenges for Parker. He got along with his classmates, his grades were good, but teachers pegged him a daydreamer. I wish we had a nickel for every recess he missed playing catch up on assignments. Most of his friends at school were girls and he had a couple of girlfriends in the neighborhood. They formed a Spice Girls club, in which a lot of time was spent planning and organizing some great event or worthy cause. At times, he would be depressed and say he was feeling overwhelmed but unable to explain why.

Parker learned a few chords on the guitar, started writing songs and picked up a camera. His brain exploded with creativity. It was as if someone turned on a bright and colorful light inside of Parker's brain, exposing a beautiful and wildly creative mind.

Teachers took notice and referred Parker to CSAS (Classen School of Advanced Studies). He applied for and was accepted into the performing arts program. Rex and I were thrilled. This was a huge opportunity. Not only would Parker be under the direction of highly acclaimed scholars and professors but he would also be learning alongside hundreds of exceptional students ranging from grades sixth through twelfth. This was great news but short lived.

Immediately Parker began to struggle in school, either the assignments were too much for him or the new friends were. This school had an excellent reputation and a long waiting list. Students not maintaining top grades were put on warning, three strikes and you were out. Parker made it two years before politely being asked to leave. His papers transferred to Taft Middle School, an inner city school that paled in comparison on *ev-er-y* level. It was a brutal move. We all took it hard for different reasons. Rex and I thought he was fully capable of doing the work at CSAS and blew a great opportunity. The move was especially rough on Parker. I'm sure he was upset about disappointing us, but more than that, he was embarrassed. The entire CSAS student body knew of only two reasons why a student would stop attending classes. #1. They died, or #2. They failed. Everybody knew Parker was alive and kickin'. He was no longer part of the elite group, forced to join what some would consider the dregs of society.

We tried to encourage Parker to go into each new school year with a 'fresh start' attitude, with better study habits and a goal of surrounding himself with good friends, only to spend the rest of the year nagging, prodding, grounding, threatening, and bribing him *just* to get a passing grade. Later Parker confided that the inner struggle he was having with his sexual identity mixed with the occasional use of drugs and alcohol led to moments of stupidity. *We all could agree to that.*

Oh, the prayers I prayed in his room when he was away at school. If it were possible, I pushed Parker to be *in* church even more. The boys were always agreeable to go, but Parker had no idea how desperately I was praying for a divine intervention; some preaching, teaching or holy bolt of lightning to strike him in the head and make him "normal".

We never heard the preacher or any teacher speak specifically against homosexuality, and as far as I know, Parker never talked to any adult in the church about his feelings. Any teaching in the youth regarding sexual matters focused primarily on purity. Girls had the promise ring and the boys learned catchy phrases like "lust says now, marriage says wait." I'm pretty sure the families in the congregation were all straight. Straight couples married in the sanctuary and that was all we saw.

When Parker was seventeen he said, "Mom, I'm gay."

I yelled at him, "You shouldn't even be thinking about this stuff! Everyone at your school thinks they're gay!" He began to make his case, reminding me of all that has happened up to now, all that has led up to this, his conclusion while I was pleading, "Do we have to decide this right now?"

I felt his frustrations grow. I knew what he was saying. Years of reading 'secret' journals fed any suspicions I had. His mannerisms and characteristics all pointed to what *little* I knew about being gay. Not that I had the 'OFFICIAL GAY CHECKLIST,' but I knew enough. I thought, *Loooord help me, Jesus.*

I had to restrain myself from shaking him, I wanted to reach into his brain and remove whatever part of it was thinking these things! I was angry at him, all of his gay friends, and *especially* the one who gave him a copy of 'Broke Back Mountain'. *Who in the hell did that?!* I was even mad at the straight ones, all the teachers that encouraged him to, "Just be yourself. You're a child of the freakin' universe." *Hell*, even the principal was gay!

I considered kicking him out of the house, We'd see how much he *knew* then! We'd see how his friends helped him *then*! I was mad at the world.

I confronted him about his journals riddled with masculine drawings, sketches, and poems expressing same sex attractions.

He protested, "This isn't about sex Mom!" It's about me and what's in my head, who I am as a person. Being gay doesn't change who I am, or what I believe. It's a part of me and sex is just a small part of it….and for the record, I'm a virgin Mom! I plan on being one for a looong time!".

Truth is, I couldn't get past the sex part of it. I

was not visualizing my son having sex. That is WRONG and NO parent should EVER do that! I was terrified of Parker actually having same-sex sex. Of course I worried about his physical health, it would be horrible if he got sick or hurt but at least we could deal with that, we have hospitals and medicine and insurance. It was the spiritual unknowns freaking me out. In my mind, same-sex sex crossed a dangerous invisible line, same-sex sex was THE big red dot that made up the very POINT of no return. I don't know exactly where the idea that Parker was going to hell came from or why it was stuck on fucking repeat in my head!

I screamed at Parker, "JUST DON'T BE GAY!"

With his fist held tight, he stood up tall and yelled back at me, "I TRIED NOT TO BE! I AM TRYING NOT TO BE! I. AM. TRRYING. NNOT. TO!"

We stood there like prisoners in the spare bedroom. The daylight was fading through the window blinds and his words hung in the air. Finally he sat back down on the floor with his back against the wall, holding his head in his hands, crying and shaken.

I plopped down on the bed and began to fidget with the laundry I was folding before all hell broke loose. Finally I spoke up about seeking some sort of counseling. Parker hesitantly agreed and we talked about that for a bit, but we couldn't point our finger at something we were both willing to whole-heartedly check out. The church was (yet again) on auto-pilot with no pastor and no youth pastor and I was not about to go to the Baptist General Convention. We settled ourselves, reaffirmed our love and agreed to talk more about this when we were not so upset. For the moment, there were no more words. We hugged. He went to his room and I went to mine.

Rex lay sleeping in our bed unaware of what just happened. I snuggled up close, intentionally trying to wake him and succeeded enough to get a, "Everything okay?" out of him.

I sighed and told him, "Parker said he's gay, again."

He took a deep breath and said, "You guys ok?"

I shrugged and replied, "I don't want him to be gay."

Rex rolled over and met me with a long hug and said, "Well, it's not what I would have chosen either…but it is what it is babe."

I whispered, "I don't want this, Rex please tell me this is not happening."

Rex propped up on his elbow, exhausted from work and this conversation. He said, "What are you gonna do about it, Sara? What can we do?" He was implying that there was in fact *nothing* anyone could do. Rex can speak volumes with just a few words and I can always count on him to be painfully honest. I have learned to ask him for help when I have trouble prioritizing or keeping things in perspective and his words always gather me up and settle me when I get scattered and undone. Then I can move on. But in this case that was not at all what I wanted to hear. I laid there restless, unable to sleep I stirred Rex again and convinced him to let me call and go see my friend Neecie from church. Rex knows Neecie and I have been long time friends, and he knows ain't nobody gonna rest until I talked this through. I pleaded with him that I needed to talk to another mother and he reluctantly agreed. Neecie met me at her front door. We sat in her living room and I told her everything. She sympathized with me and we prayed for Parker.

That night I forced myself to sleep with the help of Walgreens sleep aid, I have no idea how Parker got to sleep.

I cried so much that I woke with a migraine. With Rex already gone to work, I took Parker to school, came back home, called in sick and went to bed. Thinking I was home alone, I got out of bed to get a bottle of water from the fridge. At the same time, Travis was leaving for class and it surprised him to see me home at that time and still in my bathrobe. He took one look at my face and knew something was wrong. Before he could even ask, the floodgates opened with *"Parker says he's gaa-a-a"*.

Poor Travis tried to console me, but all he could do was stand there and look at me as if I had mustard all over my face. He did not know what to do with me. Once I got a hold of myself, I assured him to go on to class and that I just needed some rest. He was hesitant to leave me, but I insisted.

I hated that Travis saw me so upset. It only fueled the frustrations he already had towards Parker. Travis knew Rex and I were stressed about Parker screwing up at school and now this. *This* did not help Parker's case at all. It broke my heart even more to think about the growing strain between my boys. My world was upside-down and on fire. I could have laid there and died easier than see past this painful day. Today was the day that I was gonna die, I just knew it! (Drum roll please) Then Parker would be riddled with guilt and not know how much I loved him and then Travis would beat the shit out of Parker, (dramatic pause), and God only knows what Rex would do!

It would be weeks before Parker and I picked up that conversation. It would never reach the same intensity and often came in the form of a much shorter version while on the way to school or during a walk and talk after dinner. Usually our conversation would consist of me taking his spiritual temperature, and him confirming in a round-a-bout way that he was *still* gay.

For the first time as a parent, I worried about the salvation of my child. Terrifying thoughts plagued me as the left side of my brain was on high alert: WARNING! WARNING! DO NOT ENTER! STOP, DROP AND ROLL! While the right side of my brain was on the psychiatrist couch re-examining everything I had ever learned about the Gospel of Jesus Christ, my mind only knew one extreme or the other. I thought my baby was going to hell. It was impossible to gather a rational thought and any moments of clarity slipped away as fast as they came.

Picture this: My family and I are in the Ark (a.k.a. good ship salvation) with Noah (a.k.a. Jesus Christ our Lord and Savior) and the animals (a.k.a. the rest of you) (just kidding) (sorta). The boat is taking us to safety (a.k.a. paradise/heaven). The storm outside is raging (a.k.a. lost and dying world) and Parker Trent (a.k.a. my baby) is trying to open the damn window to get out!

I began to wonder if Rex and I had done something wrong. Were we bad parents? I second-guessed everything we had ever done. I knew I had been too easy on those boys, or had I been too hard? And where the hell was Rex this whole time!? We should have beaten those boys........ I had to stop and look at us as a family, our home life, what we taught our children and how we spent our time together. At that moment, I was only certain of two things. # 1. I was thankful Parker was safe at home (actually he was grounded) and #2. For my own sanity, I thought, "*I gotta figure this shit out.*"

High school came and went, and it sucked. Rex and I were like," Just pass the damn class!"

In the summer of his senior year Parker applied and was accepted to the Oklahoma Arts Institute and spent two weeks at Quartz Mountain, he came back full of artistic energy and like a hoarder he began to gather and surround himself with art supplies, treasures and oddities. He started to journal, sketch and paint. Drawing and sculpting bodies that were abstract in design. Some were plump and misshapen with pin-pricks for eyes on blank faces, others were full-figured females from neck to thigh. I remember thinking to myself, *"Why is he making naked ladies?"* But they were so interesting that I attributed it to his artistic style.

I still have those figures on a shelf at the top of the stairs. I see them every day but just this morning I noticed for the first time, a slight resemblance between the art and the artist. Whether it was intentional of Parker or not, I don't know. Perhaps it was just my imagination, but I was shaken as I considered these faceless forms were birthed out of the insecurities of a young man trying to understand his own sexual identity.

MOUNTAIN

Will I grow up - will I change too much Mama - am I
alright - what am I getting into?
I'll be alright, as long as I can stay on top of this
mountain.
If I write down - everything that I'm feeling - will they
know me - if it's only by reading?
I'll be alright, as long as I can stay on top of this
mountain.
If I find love - would I go on forever - If I leave love -
could I come back here ever?
I'll be alright as long as I can stay on top of this mountain.

Words & music by Parker Cunningham

http://www.theburnfieldcastle.com/02_mountian.m4a

Sometimes at night Parker would be on-line or on his phone with a secret friend and I could tell by his face or demeanor that the conversations were heavy. He spent hours on the front porch solving problems and sorting things out. When I would ask about it, he would lie and say he was just talking to one of his girlfriends. "She's upset over some boy at school."

Well, I guess it had been a half-truth. I later found out that through high school Parker had three relationships, one of which was long distance. The crushes, potential relationships and any breakups probably played out at night over the phone or in secret on-line. I imagined Parker pouring himself out to someone on the other end of that line, such an exciting and emotional time of his life mixed with secrets and shame.

<u>THE MILES</u>

Fear digs down deep – like a cavern excavated in me - and the
wreckage that hasn't been found - I left it for you then and I'll leave
it now – and I know I can be the needy one – and I know I can be
the needed one – and I know I could be distant - but the miles – the
miles – the miles

Joy struggles a bit – from your lips to your fingertips – and the
wreckage that hasn't been found – I left it for you then and I'll leave
it now - and I know I can be the needy one – and I know I can be the
needed one – and I know I could be distant - but the miles – the
miles – the miles.
I know I can be the needy one, and I know I can be the needed one.

Words & music by Parker Cunningham

http://www/theburnfieldcastle.com/03_the_miles.m4a

I spent nights on the internet searching for some sort of parental guide or spiritual protocol for a gay intervention. I found a few adult ministries that dealt primarily with sex and gambling addictions, and one organization that worked with persons eighteen or younger but the services offered were vague and the online reviews from parents were terrifying. Horror stories surrounded reparative therapy from both religious and secular organizations. The least threating was the PFLAG organization designed for: Parents Family and Friends of Lesbians and Gays.

TRUE STORY. Embarrassing to admit to now, but *I swear* I thought the acronym read: **Parents in Favor** of Lesbians and Gays and I figured since I was not in *favor* of "gay" anything – it was not an option. (If I had to do this all over again – I would have checked into PFLAG. It could have saved all of us a lot of grief.)

A nearby church advertised a class on, "What the bible really says about homosexuality." The speaker was a woman. She taught that God condemned Sodom and Gomorra because the people neglected the poor and needy, and that God was against homosexuality because in the sexual act the seed is wasted and at that time in history reproducing was crucial. Ok, I could understand and reason with most of what she said…but then at the end of the class she shared her testimony. She was once married to a man, years later came out as a lesbian and then divorced. Today she identifies herself to be bisexual. I left more confused than when I went in!

Barnes and Noble recommended a book on the subject. I thumbed through enough to find it was based on a true story about a mother with two children; one child died in a tragic car accident and the other was gay. She wrote about how it was easier for her to accept death over homosexuality. None of that was helpful or hopeful.

Nighttime was the absolute worst. My mind could not escape thoughts of everything I had ever heard about homosexuality, the insults "pervert", "faggot", "queer", the fear of AIDS and hate crimes. I had a boss that boasted about 'rolling fags' in high school and he didn't mean cigarettes. I imagined Parker stranded on 39th and Penn beaten and left for dead by some 'skin heads' chaining him to the bumper of a truck and then dragging him for miles. To make matters worse, throughout my life I had heard the bible stories and vague preaching against homosexuality and

I absorbed the thought that homosexuality was not only an abomination but unforgivable by God. Where did this fear for my child come from? Why was my spiritual confidence so shaken? I wrestled with scriptures that condemned and forgave. I was clinging to my faith and it was my faith that was killing me.

AUDACITY

I got promises that I'm prayin' and hopin' will fade
I got bitterness and it's whittlin' me thin
Cause my audacity is a force to be reckoned with
My audacity, audacity is–
My audacity, audacity is–
My audacity, audacity is–
My audacity, audacity is gone.

Words & music by Parker Cunningham

http://www.theburnfieldcastle.com/04_audacity.m4a

CHAPTER THREE
A LUNCH PUNCH

Photo by: Sara Cunningham

"I sucked it up for twenty years being your son. I
need you to suck it up and be my mom."

All the years of pleading with God, "Please, don't let Parker be gay. Please, don't let Parker be gay!" My worst fear was becoming a reality. Parker is gay. I imagine Parker had been praying the same prayer for most of his life. This was the burden he would try to remove from his life until today. December 23, 2010.

Today I was face to face with his sexual identity and he faced his biggest fear. Me.

Parker and I met for lunch at our favorite Indian restaurant. Comfortable at our window seat, we had just finished eating and were talking about our plans for the evening. It was a big night for Parker, playing his music at a popular night spot, the Gold Dome. When the conversation got quiet, Parker hit me with a verbal punch to the gut.

"I want you to meet someone tonight and I need you to be ok about it."

POW!

There it was. I knew what he meant. I knew this moment was coming but I was really hoping it wouldn't. Like a robot I nodded and said, "Okay." I don't remember who paid the bill or walking out of the restaurant to our separate cars. The drive back to work was surreal. Traffic lights were in my favor as I drove in slow motion. Methodically I parked my Jeep, got on the elevator, walked to the office and sat at my desk motionless with my purse on my shoulder and keys in hand. I sat there completely still, like a napkin soaking up water, slowly drinking in the reality of what – just – happened.

Parker wasn't hiding from me anymore. I could quit trying to control the outcome and we didn't have to wait any longer for this day to happen.

That evening Rex and I arrived at the Gold Dome knowing we were going to meet *someone*. We found a seat with a good view of the stage, ordered drinks and settled in. Parker was tuning his guitar and getting his mic and sound set, introduced himself to the crowd and began to play. I love Parker's music and always look forward to hearing him sing. I know the melodies and most of the words, in my mind I thought I knew what the songs were about, that was until tonight. Tonight the melodies were familiar but the words seemed different, as if he had written each song in a secret code and tonight was the big reveal. Tonight the songs told a different story.

In the course of one afternoon Parker morphed into a grown man. He carried himself on that stage with a new level of self-assurance. The afternoon had brought about a maturity that showed on his expression and sounded in his voice. That night he was singing his songs, pouring out his life stories and it was like I was hearing them for the first time. He was standing at the threshold of the rest of his life, a new beginning for Parker Trent. I imagine most parents would have been excited at this milestone. I was afraid for him.

The club was getting busy as I looked around and wondered if that *certain someone* was already here and I watched the door with anticipation as each man arrived. Parker played all of his songs and when he was done, he left the stage, greeted three friends seated across the room. Then they all came over to sit with us and Parker introduced him.

There he was, Kohl Jones, a handsome young man with striking green eyes, dark skin and dark hair. We greeted each other and arranged the table so we could all sit around it. We ordered drinks and made small talk until it was time to go. Rex and I said our good byes and that was it.

The ride home was quiet. Rex tried to make light of the evening, but he knew I had a storm a-brewin'. Depression began to creep into my bones and the next forty-eight hours are a complete blur to me. Christmas Eve dinner with friends-blur. Christmas day with extended family- bigger blur. Rex and the boys took charge of what needed to get done. If I wasn't crying or sleeping I was going through the motions pretending to be sick with the flu. Rex knew the truth and did sympathize but later told me he was surprised at how upset I was because *anybody* who knew Parker knew he was gay. That may be true, but no one, not even I knew the depth of my denial until now. Travis knew something was wrong but went along with "the flu".

Parker knew that I was upset about him and that made the situation even more heart wrenching for me. We grieved for each other's pain. As much as I grieved for myself not wanting this, I grieved for Parker and the years he spent without someone to fully confide in, no one on this earth walked alongside him. Oh, I know Rex was available and more accepting than I, and I am so thankful for that but even his acceptance of Parker was hindered because I was so wound up about it. I know that Parker had a few friends and teachers that he could talk to, but I mean, he never had the opportunity or the freedom to feel completely safe or at ease in his own skin with someone who really loved him. Only God knows the fears he faced internally and only God knows how those battles were won.

I went from grieving the loss of my dream to feeling the pain of imagining what Parker had been through even up to that day, that very hour - knowing I was hurting because of something within him he couldn't change. It was a vicious, tormenting cycle. This was the deepest sorrow I had ever known and it was two-fold, a sorrow that only he and I could share.

Even at my worst, I refused to let Parker or Travis know the full extent of my despair. I could not. Parker had already gone through so much for so long and if Travis knew the depth of my pain he would cause physical harm to Parker, I just knew it.

Finally one evening, Parker came to my room when I was 'sick' in bed. He knocked at the bedroom door and asked to come in, said he was checking on me. He came in and laid beside me for a while in the dark. He broke the silence with, "You gonna be ok, Momma?"

I said, "Yeah. I just need some time to sort things out in my head."

Then he said very lovingly, "I know Mom, please try to understand that I sucked it up for twenty years being your son and I need you now. I need you to suck it up and be my mom." Those words stung and then motivated me.

Parker and Kohl began to see each other almost every day. Kohl would usually pick Parker up at the house. He would come in and visit for a bit and then they would be gone. At first, this was awkward but with each visit, he would stay a little longer. After a few months went by, Parker expressed how happy he was and that he wanted us to get to know Kohl. He said he wanted us to be in his life, but it was up to us to decide how much. I began to see changes in Parker. He seemed at ease, more confident, outgoing and making plans for his future. I had to look beyond myself to see him this way, but there he was, comfortable with himself, his life and the way it was playing out.

My spiritual convictions never went against welcoming Kohl into our home. My only reservation, (aside from them burning in hell), was wondering how to 'love the sinner, not the sin'. How does a parent love their gay child without participating in their gay lives? How could I love everything about Parker but hate

Kohl? That hurt my head to think about and if that wasn't enough to waste my energy, I didn't know what to expect from Parker and Kohl as a couple. I mean, this was the first time we would have an official 'date' in our house and it was not a traditional 'date' situation. How would they interact with each other? Would I freak out if they held hands or sat too close together on the couch? Oh, God! What if they kissed!? We invited Kohl to dinner and none of that happened. We all behaved perfectly normal. Well, you know.

After dinner we all went outside and had a visit. Kohl teases me now, says that I asked him twenty questions. I swear I was just making conversation. It helped me to see the interaction between Parker and Kohl. They seemed to be helping each other get through the evening. Kohl was easy to talk to and I enjoyed hearing about his college days, his goals for the future and his failures from the past. I admired his work ethic as he talked about the demands of his job and I could see a resilience in him birthed from hard lessons learned. Kohl is an avid photographer and I was surprised to learn that he is a DJ and will occasionally host special events and parties. He went on to share stories from his childhood. The only child of interracial parents who proved dysfunctional separated when he was ten then lost custody of Kohl when he was thirteen. While able to keep in contact with his parents, Kohl went to live with his aunt until he turned seventeen. He got a job, his own place, started college and came out. His aunt and other family members rejected him and the church he was attending at the time asked him to leave. His father said, "I knew it all along." It took some time but things got better between them and now they are very close and have been for several years.

Kohl still talks to his mother on occasion, but wishes things were better.

As I listened to his life story I noticed 'cutting' scars on his arms and my heart broke. He went on to explain that of all the pain brought on by a broken home, and the effects of childhood depression, being gay was just the "cherry on top."

Today he says, "It is what it is." I was, and still am, so impressed with him.

Okay, so it *was* twenty questions.

That night would prove to be my first look at a new level of unconditional love. It had a name and a face. Kohl Jones.

This conversation took place in 2011. I'm sad to report in 2014 Kohl's father passed away and his mother and aunt remain distant.

THIN AIR

My five fingers – turn into ten when they're in yours
I hated flowers until I got them from you – they're the sweetest
smell I know
You came out of thin air
You came out of thin air
You got my head spinning
You came out of thin air
You keep me laughing – every night – the morning waits around on
us
You've been waiting – Just like I've been waiting – for my own white
picket fence
You came out of thin air
You came out of thin air
You got my head spinning
You came out of thin air
My five fingers – turn into ten when they're in yours.

Words & music by Parker Cunningham

http://www.theburnfieldcastle/05_thin_air.m4a

*Parker wrote this song for Kohl and sang it for the first time at the Gold
Dome.*

CHAPTER FOUR
LOSING MY RELIGION

It was all fun and games until Parker came out.

......•crickets•.

Of all the bizarre and tragic events to ever happen in this church were deeds done by those on the Sunday school roll or in a paid position. The details I would rather forget than remember; who slashed the tires on my Jeep and why they did it, how the bullet got lodged in the gym floor, or the mother that molested her teenage son. Oh, and the pastor that smoked meth in the car that he stole. I know, right? Crazy shit.

In spite of it all, I stayed for 20 years and I loved and enjoyed the people committed to and passing through that place. I have wonderful memories of prayer time in the early mornings, lock-ins with the youth, worship, and communion. I loved being a Christian; Christian radio, t-shirts, bumper stickers. Hey, if it pointed to Jesus I loved it. I enjoyed learning and talking about God, Jesus and experiencing the Holy Spirit. I had a hunger for the scriptures and was amazed when I began to learn and see parallels between the Old and the New Testaments, I have always been intrigued with biblical numbers and word studies, prophecy updates, signs of the times, online teachings, CD's anything that taught verse by verse, book by book. Every day I was excited about heaven. I was rapture ready man!....then Parker came out. I didn't stop being a Christian, loving God or all of these wonderful things, the problem was that everything came to a screeching halt when he came out. It was like the world stopped rotating.

I don't know who or how in the hell it got started, but some people in our church fellowship starting going to 'out of town' (as in, another State) conferences. Then people from 'out of town' (starts with the letter C.) started coming to our fellowship; speaking, teaching and introducing a new type of ministry. Our church leaders and people I loved were in favor of this new direction, and things started to get …weird and when things get weird in church, people split. The old people were the first to leave, then younger ones, soon Rex and Parker stopped going and that left Travis and I hanging on trying to keep the relationships with people we loved. I didn't want to be a part of a division so I tried to go with the flow. I tried to grasp the new way of thinking, I tried to understand the teachings and direction. People I loved and admired asked me, "Isn't this what I wanted? Why wasn't I playing?" They knew how much I loved the Lord and all things Spiritual, they knew how weird I could get. Hey, I even considered going 'out of town' (Jed and Granny Clampett moved there) in an effort to understand this obvious move of the Spirit. I thought I could get it. I wanted what they had and I was desperate to stay in the fellowship until some started referring to demons as 'critters' while others were looking for floating feathers, gold dust and angels in the friggin' balcony.

SHIT.

I needed those people, but they were on the train leaving the station and I couldn't go with them, and that put a space between us, which didn't give the ones I love the opportunity to be with us during our time of crisis. It could be that no one knew what was happening at my house or they were too deep into their own crisis to come and counsel us. In my heart I secretly wanted my church family to come to my house and minister to us tenderly, to reaffirm their love *and* God's love toward us and especially to Parker.

Perhaps my church family didn't know how to approach us. After all, we were the ones to leave them. Either way, the church split, combined with what we were going through at home, put a great strain on our relationships and the silence hurt. I know for a fact that if any one person in that congregation that knew us and loved us could have offered us one ounce of hope or encouragement in our situation regardless of the split – they would have busted our door down to tell us so. I remember times in the past, be it celebration or crises the church poured into our home with great expressions of love, comfort and compassion and *that* is what I wanted for us. That is what we needed now. Even as vague as homosexuality was at Crestwood I still felt like we were now unapproachable. Whether it was ignorance or judgment, intentional or not the silence was brutal.

Rex and I process things differently, he didn't want to talk about it and that's all I want to do, I have no filter – I need to discuss things – work things out and even though we agreed that this was Parkers personal business and if he wanted someone to know, he would be the one to tell them. Not that we were gonna take out a full page ad about it, but for me personally, there were people in my life I wanted and needed to talk to about it.

I found myself trying to confide with people within my circle. My life at that time revolved around my faith and church so that meant the majority of the people in my life were *'good Christian folk'.* I have always felt a sense of camaraderie among the *'brethren,'* you know, people of like mind.

One friend reassured me that Parker was just trying to get a reaction out of me, and not to worry about it. Another friend sympathized with me as much as she could but she "didn't want her son around *that.*" As time went on and word got out family members made it clear that they loved Parker but his partner would never be welcome in their home. Another pointed out "It's not natural, even the animals know that!" Others assured us that Parker being gay would never change anything between us, but our interactions were different and became less and less.

As Parker was walking out of his closet, we were walking into ours and *everything* changed. When and if I shared my family secret, I was met with sympathy and prayers of compassion for me as a mother, for me as a *sister in Christ* and that was wonderful. But all too often, the prayers of the saints turned into heavy stacking stones... "Lord, forgive Parker," ... "change Parker," ... "gates of hell," ... "love the sinner, hate the sin," ... "remove the bondage,"... "restore what the enemy has taken," ... "he exchanged the truth for a lie," ... "he's been blinded by the lies of the enemy,"... "remove the lust of the flesh,"

My heart sank with every prayer.

Did my fellow Christians not know the years I had pleaded, prayed, and begged God with those very words!? No one prayed more than I did for my son -no one!

Wait a minute, I take that back. I'm *pretty* sure Parker prayed the gay away more than I did and let's not forget that Parker had accepted Jesus Christ as *his* very own Lord AND Savior AND had been baptized.

Hate the sin, love the sinner sounds real good if you're on the loving end of that equation, but if you're on the sinner's side of that prayer it feels dehumanizing and condescending or at least it did to me. All of a sudden, my son was the outcast stuck in a perpetual state of sin condemned to hell. I wondered if my brothers and sisters in Christ were ministering to me with words they thought I wanted or expected to hear? Would these be their prayers over Parker if he had reached out to them when he was feeling alone and confused? Good Lord! I'm grown and straight and these prayers condemned me! I would not want any of this for Parker, not for anyone.

Insult and injury came in all directions, for

years I was the oldest member in a kickboxing class. I loved the workout and admired the instructor as a godly man who had a heart for young people. One night after class a young girl who knew me and about Parker, pulled me aside and discreetly confided with me that her brother (who was also in the class), just came out and that the whole family was in an uproar. My heart immediately understood and we both began to cry. Our instructor seeing that we were upset rushed over and inquired, she, not wanting to point out her brother, reluctantly shared "I found out someone is gay," and without missing a beat the instructor shook his head like he was disgusted and said, "Awww man, the gates of hell are *wiiide* open for 'em."

I gave our instructor a hard look and walked my kickboxing friend to her car and that was the last class I went to, mostly because that hurt me, and I just got lazy.

Another injury came while visiting friends who live in the country. They have a little barn on their property that they recently remodeled into an apartment. It was a beautiful space. I commented that it would make for a great bed and breakfast, and that they should rent it out. They nodded in agreement and said

"Yeah, but we probably won't, because then we'd have to rent to *those guys.*"

I said, "What guys?"

They whispered, "You know… *the gays.*"

I said, "Oh..those guys."

It was hard hearing these things but even more upsetting to me was that even though these people didn't know about Parker, they knew me and still felt comfortable enough to say such things.

Tired of seeing me upset Rex said, "How about we let this be their problem now, not ours."

I began to question everything I believed in. Even the friendships that meant so much to me seemed to be in limbo. The phone quit ringing; no more prayer chain, no communion, no study, no more lunch dates and I quit going to ladies night. I felt like my eyes were being forced open and I was being plunged into a new reality. *I seriously thought about hanging a huge banner outside our front door: WELCOME TO THE REAL WORLD!*

It took everything in me just to get up, get dressed and go to work. I could hardly complete a sentence without crying. My mind was consumed with thoughts about Parker. I was fearful he might leave town, hurt himself or worse consider suicide. I mourned the life I had imagined for Parker; dating a nice girl, getting married, starting a family. I feared that his being gay would overshadow everything that was good about him. Would he be treated, looked at or talked about differently.

My worries became a daily reality as the entire world was focusing in on the equal rights controversy. Everyone was barking about Chick-Fil-A, Hobby Lobby, Boy Scouts and the Duck Dynasty debate. There was no escaping it. It was all over the news, my FaceBook feed, even discussions in the break room. All I could see was conflict between Gays and Christians and all that I could hear was the hatred hurled towards my son. I took it all personal. Each insult was like a punch to my gut. I had never felt so alienated from the church or society. It was heart wrenching as I began to realize that I was experiencing now what Parker and so many others like him have most of their lives. I'll never forget the pain I felt when I heard a preacher I greatly admired liken the gay community to child molesters, perverts and those involved in bestiality Really?! That is not my son! How could anyone make such accusations? That was the day I took down the wooden cross that hung from my rearview mirror. I felt guilty by association.

I was in my own private hell, certain the discouragement was growing inside of me like a cancer. I was torn between my love for him and this idea that he was going against everything holy. How could I accept something about him that the church, friends and some family found morally wrong? I knew that I did not want to alienate Parker and if I could not change him, I was desperate to find a way to understand and accept him and even more desperate to resolve the spiritual conflict in my mind. Why would or *how* could anyone *choose* a life that guaranteed hell on earth in forms of being disowned by family, abandoned by friends, alienated by society, beaten by gay bashers AND THEN declared an abomination by the church AND THEN be thrown into the fiery furnace!

Years of information, life experiences and any spiritual understandings I had about God's love and grace for us were scattered on the floor like grains of sand and no matter how hard I tried, I could not gather a single grain of reason. I had never ever doubted the security or salvation for my children through the work of the cross and the blood of Jesus Christ. We are

Christians, we believe the Gospel and the promise of heaven and that was it. Period. Suddenly I was getting the message that-*that* was not enough?¡ Now we have conditions?¡ WTFrick? As if the cross was not enough¡? Then, everything I thought I knew about God's grace meant nothing. It was as if all of the pages in my bible had been torn out, except for the ones that condemned homosexuality, and the word homosexual had been replaced with Parker's name.

The more I tried to renew my spiritual strength within the church or with my online studies the more discouraged I became. Like a ticking time bomb, I never knew when or in what form the condemnation against the gay community would come, but it came. I went into the study hungry and left hurting. Intentional or not, any undertone of judgment worked like a shut off valve in my head. If I detected even a hint of hells fire, my ears just turned off. Judgment was to hope, like drops of poison to water.

I started to rationalize, trying to gain understanding and perspective of the Spiritual situation. I mean, just how bad could things get, right? *What if Parker is gay but vows never to have same-sex sex? What if he did have same-sex sex, but only once¡*

and then never again? What if he stays gay, marries a woman but still desires a man. Or wait, could being married to a woman make him straight? What if he marries a man and is faithful to him until death? Can he be gay and still believe in God? What if being gay is not a choice? What if he can't fight it? What if he kills himself?! What if the church has got this all wrong?...but...then again, what if the church is right? Oh God!

At night I would plead with God for an answer. I was sick and tired of the confusion I had between God's grace and the message of condemnation from the church. DOES THE BLOOD OF JESUS CHRIST COVER IT OR NOT? This was crucial information that I needed to know, not only for my own sanity. It was a matter of life or death for my son!

I would pray: Give it to me straight God. Is he gonna make it or is this a double death sentence? At this point I don't care if it was his choice to be gay or if he was born gay. The only thing that matters to me at this moment is whether or not he is going to hell. Period. Forget any blessings here on earth, forget the crowns in heaven. I just need to know if he's gonna make it through the gates! Spare me the labor pains, show me the baby! I'd be happy with a loop-hole at this point! I can't take another speculation, I don't want another debate, I just need a simple YES[ ] or NO [ ] Put a check in the box God 'cause IF IT'S TRUE THAT PARKER IS GOING TO HELL FOR BEING GAY THEN I NEED TO STAND AND FIGHT FOR HIM LIKE MY HAIR IS ON FIRE!! AND IF IT'S NOT…. THEN… well if it's not …I need to settle the hell down.

I was desperate for understanding… and sleep.

GHOST TOWN

Oh sun, you haven't been shining like you used to in my old, old eyes.
Oh moon, your babies ain't twinkling like they're holdin' something back from me.

But when this ghost town is laughin' and shining - I'll make it up to you – and when our children are singin' hallelujah – I'll make it make it up to you.

Oh earth, your body's been shakin', you're quivering, quaking like I've done somthin' wrong.

Oh fields, you ain't been growing and I don't know if rain is coming soon.

But when this ghost town is laughin' and shining - I'll make it up to you – and when our children are singin' hallelujah – I'll make it make it to up you.

Oh house, you sure been leakin', floorboards creakin', I've been losin' sleep.

Oh sky, you haven't been sharing, you think I don't care but I've been cryin' out.

But when this ghost town is laughin' and shining - I'll make it up to you – and when our children are singin' hallelujah – I'll make it make it up to you.

Words & music by Parker Cunningham

http://www.theburnfieldcastle.com/06_ghost_town.m4a

CHAPTER FIVE
GLIMMERS OF HOPE

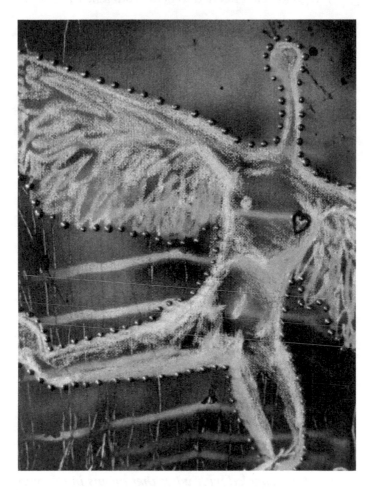

The fruit of the spirit is love. Galatians 5:22

I was desperate for a deeper understanding that would go beyond my preconceived idea that if you're gay you go to hell. I needed to hear from a heart of someone who really knew what I was going through with my son and my faith. I needed someone to speak to me about the power of love and the gift of grace and not a single thing more.

* **JENNIFER KNAPP** immediately came to mind. No, I don't know her personally, but I love her music. She is a long time Christian artist who recently announced that she's gay. You can imagine the upset in the Christian music industry. I found the following quote: *"The struggle I've had has been with the church, acknowledging me as a human being, trying to live the spiritual life that I've been called to, in whatever ram shackled, broken, frustrated way that I've always approached my faith. I still consider my hope to be a whole human being, to be a person of love and grace. So it's difficult for me to say that I've struggled within myself, because I haven't. I've struggled with other people. I've struggled with what that means in my own faith. I have struggled with how that perception of me will affect the way I feel about myself."*

She had been signed under a new label and recently released a new CD called 'Letting Go.' I went out, bought the CD, gave it a listen in my Jeep and cried as she sang about her struggle and faith. It was the first time I thought that a person could be gay and Christian. That gave me **HOPE.**

⁕ **EFFIE** is a longtime friend of mine. We don't get to see each other much. She's a young mother with a big family, a lot younger than me but like an old soul. She once told me that people with secrets are drawn to her. We met for coffee and then stopped at a nearby park. We visited for a while and at one point near the end of our conversation she looked at me and said something like, "so, what's going on with Parker? Like, you know he's gay, right?"

I'm embarrassed to think about what my face must have looked like at that very moment. I was still trying to wrap my head around the situation, let alone talk about it. She had no way of knowing that I had been so upset, feeling alienated from some of my own family and the church. Then she said something like, "You know Jesus still loves him, right? And it's all gonna be okay, right?"

Her words were like honey. I cry a little when I remember that day. Effie was the first person to ask me about Parker straight up. She was one of the few friends to accept Parker for who he was, and then be sensitive towards us as a family as we walked this out. She was the first human being to show me God's love in the form of **ACCEPTANCE.**

* **MISSY** and her husband Shawn started Bohemian church when Parker was in high school. He became friends with several of the young people there, we visited several times and fell in love with the small congregation. The church dissolved when the family moved and I lost contact with them until today. Their son Gabriel, a young folk singer reminiscent of Bob Dylan, was set to play his music at a nearby coffee shop so I went to take a listen and was hopeful I'd see Missy. Gabe had already started playing and sounded amazing when I walked into the coffee shop. I scanned the room, saw Missy standing in a corner and instantly my mind went to a time when I was soaring in my faith instead of struggling in this pit of despair. Like an old homeless man on the street seeing a childhood friend, I longed for 'the good old days.' I worked my way to her,

grabbed her arm, dragged her into the bathroom, slammed and locked the door so that no one could see what was about to go down. I faced her and then hugged her tight. Before I could even utter a sound I sank my head into her shoulder and began to sob uncontrollably. It was a snotty ugly groaning from the gut kind of cry. I finally managed to get broken words out, "Paaa-rkeeer...(groan)....gagaaay," and that was all she needed. She just hugged me and let me cry. I don't remember any words of wisdom or prayer; just that she was the first person to receive all of my sorrow and like a sponge, she took it all in without any hesitation. She gave me **COMFORT.**

* **A MISSION TRIP FRIEND.** I met a woman on a mission trip in Mexico. At the time, she was the first person outside of my immediate family that shared my secret. We walked a path around the small hotel parking lot as she told me about her family. Starting with how she and her husband grew up and married in a small town, serving for years in a small church and then having a son born and raised in the same small town and church. Devastation came when their son graduated high school, told them he was gay, took a job in another state and moved there with his partner. She and her husband immediately followed him and begged him to come home, he refused. Days later the church elders traveled to see him, they pleaded with him and warned him of the Spiritual consequences. Still he refused. She said her husband became so distraught that he tried to commit suicide. It would be months before their son would return calls and when he did, he forbid any mention of the church or him coming home. A year or so later, her son died. (I never knew how he died, just that he died in the hospital). I was able to attend the funeral. My heart ached for her and her husband as I watched the slide show that celebrated his young life. After the service, my mission trip friend shared from one of her last moments together with her son. She said, "He stared into the distance and then lifted his arms as if to embrace Jesus," she said that moment gave her great peace.

When Parker came out, I called my mission trip friend and told her everything. I asked if she had any words of wisdom for me, she said, "Love him and make your home a safe place." That gave me a **FOUNDATION.**

* **MY NEIGHBORS.** Robert and Kathy live in the same neighborhood and we are all mutual friends. Kathy loves to garden and she maintains the neighborhood flowerbeds. One Sunday in early Spring she invited Robert and I to help pull weeds. I don't know this for sure, but I think Kathy and Robert were in cohorts that day because she knew I was upset about Parker and the church split and it just so happens that Robert is a gay Christian. They were trying to help me feel better and I appreciate that, the day would prove both painful and pivotal.

Painful was the realization that I had been looking to and even expecting the church to meet my spiritual needs. Looking back, I believe God orchestrated that Sunday with Robert and Kathy. He knew what I needed could never come from the church or the circles I ran with, at least not at that time.

Pivotal in the fact that on that day I began my spiritual journey from the church to the gay community and walking with me, were my neighbors. Robert, a gay Christian and Kathy, a person who doesn't consider herself very spiritual. We entered into a **FELLOWSHIP.**

<u>YOU GOT HEART</u>

You got heart as big as the sun and it shines just as brightly and it is open - open just like door and it never closes - well I can hear it beating right out of your chest, you got heart, you got heart, you got heart and it beats like a drum.

You got heart that never grows colder like a sunflower in summer and it sings - oh it sings like an angel's choir and it moves just like wildfire - well I can hear it beating right out of your chest, you got heart, you got heart, you got heart and it beats like a drum.

Words & music by Parker Cunningham

http://theburnfieldcastle.com/07_you_got_heart.m4a

CHAPTER SIX
A GAY WEDDING

Photo provided by, Starving Dog *Photography*.

I'm with you.

Are you sitting down? Would you believe I encouraged Parker to move in with Kohl? By now the two were practically inseparable. Parker wasn't staying out all night or being disrespectful about their relationship. My reasoning was this; he's twenty-one and clearly making his own decisions and there was no getting that cat back in the bag. Honestly, I was okay with the move. I felt like it needed to happen and I knew it was going to happen, so "fly" I say, "be free."

Once it was decided, it happened in a flash. Keep in mind that this was Parker's only home. He lived in the same bedroom for twenty-one years. Twenty-one years of shi-tuff moved out the front door in less than an hour! Wow!

The minute that front door closed, I immediately missed Parker terribly. All of those feelings of loss came rushing back to me. Suddenly I was in the middle of a horrible melt down and the memories flooded into every room. I could see him as a toddler running through the dining room wearing only his diaper, then in the living room with his brother building forts out of couch cushions or watching cartoons together on Saturday mornings, doing homework at the kitchen table, sitting on the porch waiting for Dad to get home, bath time, story time, bed time – oh my gosh! It was awful how much I missed that boy. After a week or so I settled down and it helped when we made Sunday nights family night.

I always look forward to Sunday. We make dinner, sit around and visit or watch a movie. It's a time that everyone is together and I like that.

The next few months allowed us to settle into this new family dynamic. In-laws, extended family and friends have now had time to face the reality that Parker is gay and in a serious relationship. Rex and I knew that if we wanted to be a part of Parker's life we would have to welcome Kohl and we did. It's not like we had a family meeting to discuss how we were going to be accepting. It was something that just happened as we spent time together. I like how Travis said it, "I would prefer Parker not to be gay, but he's my brother and I don't want to be an asshole." We all had to search ourselves, feel our way through this new phase of the family. Our immediate family has been supportive of Parker and have welcomed Kohl into their homes. I'm sure they did some soul searching on the matter too, and I am so thankful they have walked with us through this. I could not imagine our lives without their love and support. The more time we spent together, the more accustomed all of us became to seeing Parker and Kohl together. It was a series of firsts. The first time we all went out to dinner, I wondered if people would notice us as a 'blended' family and not because Kohl is black. Or the first time a friend was visiting at the house and Parker and Kohl were on their way over. When my friend realized they were about to meet the boys as a couple she leaned into me and squinted her eyes and said, "They aren't gonna kiss are they?" I was able to handle that question gracefully *only* because I wondered the same thing at one time! (Why do we expect them to always be groping each other? – Who does that?)

Once we got past our own insecurities, we could see them for who they are as individuals and then as a couple. It was reassuring to see the boys work at their relationship, starting out in a small apartment, fixing it up the way they wanted, working and paying the bills, respecting, depending on and caring for each other. Also, seeing the relationships that were being built up and established around them. Friends, Co-workers, and other couples who they chose to spend time with helped me to see the kind of adult/couple they are and were becoming.

Their social circle is full of some of the most genuine hardworking, caring people I have ever met. As a parent it's wonderful to see your children have good friends, knowing they have a network of people that will have their best interest in mind and vice-versa. Even in the ordinary things like hearing them talk about their grocery list helped me see efforts they were making to have a good relationship. They make each other happy and we enjoy Kohl and what he brings to our family.

Fast forward a couple of years, and a phone call from Kohl wanting to meet with Rex and I. We weren't totally surprised when Kohl called and said that he had something important to ask us. We were learning that Kohl is a traditionalist at heart and I like that. He was letting us know of his plan to ask Parker to marry him. I know what you're thinking – what about a gay wedding is traditional? We gave him our blessing and then started planning for a party in our back yard to celebrate Kohl's birthday and introduce some new music he and Parker had been working on. They call themselves, 'Bandit and the Blackbird' (Kohl is the Bandit and Parker is Blackbird, I think.) Kohl's plan was to ask Parker to marry him at the party.

Travis made a huge canvas banner with the words 'Bandit and the Blackbird' and he drew a Bandit mask and a Blackbird in flight and hung it across the back fence. He hid about a hundred little plastic balls that contained LED multi colored lights all around the backyard, plus someone loaned us a party laser light show box that made for an amazing light show. The weather was perfect, and the music sounded great. Kohl played a type of techno, dub step, beat box, rap scratcher...(Ok, so I don't know what you call it) It's a really cool sound and Parker sang to the beat. It sounded like some new age modern stuff. I was so impressed with each one of those boys. If someone told me that our back yard would be host to such a gathering, I would have _never_ believed it. Both Parker and Kohl dressed the part of Blackbird and the Bandit. The crowd was great and on their feet until the last song played. Everyone gathered around, Kohl took the mic and dropped down on one knee and proposed.

Parker was thrilled and said, "Yes!" We celebrated until the lights went out. Actually, we partied until the cops came and told us we were being too loud.

The date was set for September 7th. 2013. Rex

and I made ourselves available and were glad that Parker and Kohl already had an idea of what they wanted the wedding to look like as we had no idea, so we followed them around shopping and helped make decisions when asked.

At the time of this writing same sex marriage is not legal or recognized in the state of Oklahoma so they decided to have the wedding in our back yard, reception at a local art studio and then get legally married in Seattle.

Plans were coming together smoothly and quickly, we spent weeks transforming the back yard, adding pretty river rock boarders, planting assorted flowers here and there, picking up dog poop. Travis built and stained a two level platform and braced three antique white doors for a backdrop. Then he added an old chandelier that hung at the center of the doors, it was beautiful. That boy has been a constant force behind the scenes. No matter what the task he steps up and goes beyond my expectations. He can be so hard headed, but his heart is always willing to go and do and be whatever I need, and I respect and admire him for these things.

The cake was ordered, chairs rented and

ironically we bought most of the decorations from Christian department stores. As the invitations went out, I secretly thought the list could have been a little longer if this were a 'straight' wedding. Congratulation cards came in the mail from Rex's extended, more conservative family and that was a nice surprise.

Parker and Kohl never lost their confidence or vision for the wedding and that was reassuring, but I still had my moments where I would feel overwhelmed. One afternoon at work I began to feel anxious and I took a break from work and went outside for a walk. Thumbing through my phone I saw the 800 number for a helpline that was offered through a radio ministry I listened to regularly. On a whim I called and told the long distance preacher that my son is gay and now engaged to his partner and that I was feeling overwhelmed. The preacher said, "Continue to love your son, but never allow his partner into your house and certainly don't attend the wedding." I hung up feeling totally deflated. What was I expecting? I immediately regretted calling. The conversation would stay with me, but it was the last time I sought advice from church family or any religious organization.

A few days later I found myself in the laundry

room staring out the window trying to imagine the wedding and a feeling of absolute dread came over me. I felt like I was stuck in the middle of a road and I had no idea which way to go. Then I had me a laundry room conversation:

> Me: *God I don't think I can handle any of this.*
> God: *Girl, you got this.*
> Me: *What do I do?*
> God: *Celebrate Parker.*
> Me: *How do I do that?*
> God: *Love what he loves.*
> Me: *.......Okay, let's go.*

In my mind I imagined Parker and I on the Yellow Brick Road. Standing arm and arm we look at each other and I give him a nod of approval and say, "Okay, let's go!" And we went on down that road.~I say we moved on down, moved on down the road~.

Weeks flew by and soon the house was buzzing with preparations. Parker bought several yards of fabric, ranging in texture and different shades of white and gold. He cut them into long strips and we hung them like garland through the trees. It was beautiful like something you'd see on a Stevie Nicks album cover. The stage and backdrop that Travis made were set in place as well as the chairs. Kathy surprised us with flowers from her garden, a simple act for her but to me it was a beautiful public display of affection and acceptance towards another human being. The back yard never looked so good, before we knew it rehearsal dinner came and went and the day had arrived.

The boys arranged for Amy, a longtime friend to preside over the wedding and just like they had rehearsed the music started to play and she came and stood on the small platform and directed everyone (about 120 people, just sayin') to stand. The wedding party approached and gathered at the small stage, Kohl followed suite, then I walked Parker 'down the aisle' where he met and stood beside Kohl and they both turned to face Amy. Everyone was seated and got quiet. She began by talking directly to Parker. She shared about how they met and the qualities she admired about him. Then she faced Kohl and did the same for him. Next she spoke to them as a couple and encouraged them together. She addressed the crowd and inspired us collectively to support and honor this union. The boys read their vows and then Rex joined them and closed with a prayer:

Lord, thank you for Kohl and his love for Parker. I pray that they continue to lift each other up, be accountable and helpers to each other. Lord that they will continue to seek You and bless You. Reveal Yourself to them as only You can. Bless them, protect them and surround them with people who will love, encourage and pour into them. Amen

Rex was seated as Amy told them to kiss and when they did, she announced them ....I think King and Queen? After a warm round of applause, we were dismissed from the backyard wedding and then gathered at a nearby art studio for the reception that included a slide show of the boys that played along with some of their favorite music. We served cake and fruit and toasted with pink champagne. The boys celebrated and we were all amazed at the financial generosity and emotional support from family, friends and acquaintances. See? Traditional for the most part.

I'M WITH YOU

You painted me happy in the colors of everything that I wanted and I followed the sway of the water to you – I read your fingertips like a map to where I wanted to be – I followed them to find you here to say I'm with you, till the sun it just won't shine – till the flowers just won't bloom – until Jesus takes me home – I'm with you – I'm with you - I'm with you.

You loved me perfectly with ten thousand songs and rhythms that I can't describe I love the sound of your every breath - I found myself falling harder and faster and ever in love with you – your words are sweet like honey to me - when you say I'm with you, till the sun it just won't shine – till the flowers just won't bloom – until Jesus takes me home – I'm with you – I'm with you - I'm with you.

Words & music by Parker Cunningham

http://www.theburnfieldcastle.com/08_im_with_you.m4a

CHAPTER SEVEN
WHAT'S IN MY HEAD

Lord, let my understanding return to me.

I have admitted on more than one occasion that I would rather live a life of delusion than believe my son was going to hell for being gay. I have also prayed on more than one occasion to be a woman of good understanding. Trust. I have walked a very fine line. That is why this chapter might suck for you, 'cause I'm gonna try to explain in 25 words or less per point (not gonna happen), what was rolling around in my head during this very difficult time in my life. These are not all of the thoughts that brought me to a place of peace on the matter of homosexuality, but these were most re-occurring. I had to re-examine what I believed and hold it in light of what I was learning right now, and you bible scholars, don't debate or dismiss the scriptures if you feel they are out of context, these are my perceptions formed from years of various studies. These 'points' are what have influenced and stuck with me, they give me rest and that makes them mine. Besides this is my book. I write what I want.

o **John 3:16** For God so loved the world, that he gave his only begotten Son, that **whosoever** believes in him shall not perish but have everlasting life. (25 words BAM)

I could stop right here…....

o **Let Each Man Be Determined In His Own Mind And Work Out His Own Salvation. Based on Romans 14.5 / Philippians 2.12.** I believe that Parker searched the heart of God before he could be at peace with being gay. I believe that he and God ironed out all the details on this one and that Parker worked out his own salvation. Like every human could and should. Furthermore, having a solid opinion is important, but we should not make another man stumble over it. What is holy to one man may not be to the other, my convictions are not yours and vice-versa. When I was young someone told me I was offensive to God because my hair is short and that the Baptist and Catholic Church were false religions. That shit messed me up when I was younger. You can't do that to people.

o **No One Knows The Heart Of A Man Or The Mind Of God.** I don't and neither do you or those guys. Period.   We will never have the final word on God's truth. (count em' 20.)

o **The Secret Things Belong To The Lord.** I believe that there is a dynamic to homosexuality that we don't understand and we won't understand it until we get to heaven. The secret things belong to the Lord and we don't have to know everything. If we did, we would just argue about it.

o **The Characteristics of God.** Both male and female attributes are outlined so powerfully and beautifully throughout the bible and the fact that each one of us are created in the image of God, it is not so hard for me to believe that a person could embody the essence of both male and female, some more than others. Just watch the Discovery channel. You'll see.

I should stop here......

o   **The Principle of First Mention.** When my depression was at its worst, I noticed something strange about the muscles in my face. It was like they shifted into a position I had never felt before and one day I actually examined my face in the mirror and thought *"so, this is what depression looks like"* and I remembered a bible study in the book of Genesis about Cain and Able, remember that one? Cain was jealous of Able's offering and the bible says "his face was downcast" then Cain went on to kill his brother. In this study I was learning about a theory called 'Principle of First Mention'. According to this theory, when a word or concept is mentioned in the bible for the first time, it sets the definition for its uses from then on. So in studying the word: DOWNCAST in light of what was happening in the story of Cain and Able it not only paints a picture of the word, it expounds the meaning of it. Stay and think with me: Cain compared offerings= JUDGMENT/ CONDEMNATION. Cain got depressed= DOWNCAST/ DISCOURAGED. Cain killed Able= DEATH. The more I thought about the lesson, the more I realized that internally I was judging/condemning Parker and externally it was causing this new expression on my face. Oh! I didn't want to kill Parker, but my face was definitely downcast. Now every time I feel my face make *that* expression *(and I know it well!)*, I check myself and find that it happens every time I dwell on comparing myself to, or being jealous of another person. This even applies to dwelling on how others might compare or judge me. I believe there is a link between judgment and depression that causes real damage both physically and spiritually.

o **Pictures of Grace:** In the Old Testament Moses stood on holy ground, what did God instruct him to do?

Remove the sandals from his feet. Exodus 3:5. Now fast forward to the New Testament: When the prodigal son returned home. What did his father do? He put sandals on his feet. Luke15:22 Why? Because Moses speaks of the law, while the prodigal son speaks of grace. The 'Law' is not interested in people. It lacks soul. (pun intended.)

o **More Pictures of Grace:** Because I can't let you forget about the Old Testament story of Cain and Abel. After Cain kills Able, God comes to him and says: The blood of your brother cries out to Me. Genesis 4:10. What does Abel's blood cry? It's a message of condemnation and judgment. Now again, fast forward to the New Testament book of Hebrews 12:24 ... the blood of Jesus speaks of better things than the blood of Abel. What does the blood of Jesus cry? It cries, "Forgiven." Aren't those beautiful pictures? So many nights I wrestled between the Law that goes against homosexuality and the forgiveness from God's grace that pardons it. These 'pictures' are what I meditated on. I looked at them constantly and they remind me that God's love is enough and that forgiveness and grace trumps any law every time.

o **The Bible.** It's simply profound and profoundly simple. Genesis Chapter Five is the genealogy of Christ - Adam through Noah. Thirty-two versus of b*oooo*ring, until you do a word study on the names. Check this out:

> Adam = **MAN**
> Seth = **APPOINTED**
> Enosh = **SUBJECT TO DEATH**
> Kenan = **SORROWFUL**
> Mahalalel = **FROM THE PRESENCE OF GOD**
> Jared = **ONE COMES DOWN**
> Enoch = **DEDICATED**
> Methuselah = **DYING HE SHALL SEND**
> Lamech = (to the) **POOR AND LOWLY**
> Noah = **REST AND COMFORT**

It's the Gospel. The Good News right there! Do you see it? Amazing! The bible is full of these wonderful pictures and illustrations. So my thinking is this, if God can spell out the Gospel with names in one boring chapter, how much more could we be gleaning or worse, how much more are we missing in the fullness of letters, words and their meaning.

o **If we gonna hinge salvation** or even imply that God's favor would be lost on the WORD or ACT of homosexuality than let it be so for the final commandment from God, which is **that we love one another** John 13:34, or the last words recorded in Scripture **may God's grace be on all people** Rev. 22:21.

I *really* should stop right here…..

o **Paving the Way.** The growing acceptance of the gay community could be paving the way for bible prophecy to be fulfilled. The bible gives mention that the antichrist will be a man in high authority and that he will not be a 'lover of women' which (to me) *could* mean he's in love with himself, he's a womanizer or maybe, just maybe, he's gay. Hold on people …I'M NOT SAYING YOU'RE THE ANTICHRIST IF YOU'RE GAY, (or any of those other things). I'm saying that we are at a point in our history where a person that is gay could be elected president, pope or some third world leader and perhaps the growing acceptance and support of the gay community is God's way of paving the way for this particular 'antichrist' prophecy to be fulfilled.

o **Where In The heck** did I get that idea? Consider this – the bible also prophesied that Israel would become a state in just one day, in which it did on

May 14, 1948. It has been suggested that the world and world leaders had deep sympathy for the Jewish people due to the atrocities of the Holocaust and this world event paved the way for the 'one day State' prophecy to be fulfilled.

o **Sinners Saved by Grace.** I get that and I am so thankful. But all too often the words "we are all sinners saved by grace" are followed with "homosexuality is no different than those caught up in addiction, adultery, gluttony" and so on. Of all the sins I've been forgiven, being straight is something that I have never struggled with, been convicted of, or required forgiveness for. Therefore I have come to the conclusion that homosexuality, be it by birth or choice is no more of a sin than me being straight.

You still reading?

o **Education.** I read about being gay, being a gay Christian, being straight and loving someone who's gay. I cannot stress how important this step was. Reading up on what's happening between the Church and the Gay community was a reality check that helped me find what I think is a healthy balance between the two. I would highly recommend the following:

Torn: Rescuing the Gospel from the Gays-vs.-Christians Debate by Justin Lee

Pray the Gay Away: The Extraordinary Lives of Bible belt Gays by Bernadette C. Barton

The Children are Free: Reexamining the Biblical Evidence on Same-Sex Relationships by Rev. Jeff Miner, John Tyler Connoley

Stranger at the Gate: To Be Gay and Christian in America by Mel White

No Exceptions: A Gay Christian's Guide by Victoria M. St Christopher

Found Tribe: Jewish coming out stories. Edited by Lawrence Schimel

Born This Way: Real Stories of Growing Up Gay by Paul Vitagliano

You know when you meet someone for the first time, they start talking and seem perfectly normal and then the more they talk the more you think they might have a screw lose? But you let them keep talking just to see how long they'll go, and you make that mental note to yourself, *"Walk the other way next time I see her coming down the hall"*....well that's how I'm feeling right now, like I'm the only one talking. Truth is, I hesitated in sharing these thoughts with you, not because I'm embarrassed of the way I think or what I believe, but because sharing my personal thoughts on such a sensitive subject makes me vulnerable to you. But I had to. How could I not share the very things that saved me from a slow and painful death.

P.S. Behold in the Greek means Yahoo! Rev. 1:7.

<u>LOCUST</u>

You got a cigarette lit, I got a cup of wine, and yet the words don't
seem to come any easier
We walk around the water and yet we both just know that we were
long since dead like locust hulls on bark
And if you know I'll know - but if you don't I'll go - and if you say
we're through - then I will know I've won – but if you smile
nothing's been done
The moon hides in sweet hesitation, she won't show her face tonight
and yet the waves are crashin' for the both of us
I look at the scars on your fingers, you hear my unspoken words but
everyone is saying things behind our backs
And if you know I'll know - but if you don't I'll go - and you say
we're through - then I will know I've won – but if you smile - but if
you smile - but if you smile, nothing's been done.

Words & music by Parker Cunningham

http://www.theburnfieldcastle.com/09_locust.m4a

CHAPTER EIGHT

GOOD NIGHT, LOVE YOU.

Art work by: Rex Cunningham

Perfect love casts out all fear. 1 John 4:18

Today came with two major events. The first event is that I started this, the last chapter of the book. Trust me, this is major. You have no idea how hard it's been to get what's in my heart and head on this paper. I knew from the beginning that the last chapter of this book would be titled 'Good night, Love you.' 'Love you' are words that my family has tacked onto every 'good bye and good night' for as long as I can remember and I like that, but I didn't know how I would end this chapter, until today. The second major event is that Rex and I went to the Pride Parade and stood in support of our son, his husband and the gay community at large. All day I prayed that God would give me something that would lend direction to this final chapter and that He would help me better understand the significance of the Parade but even more than those things, I prayed that I would experience the presence of the Lord in a practical and powerful way. I needed a picture or an illustration of the Lord's favor. I wanted to see Him there.

Until today, I didn't understand the symbols used to represent the Gay Community, you know the Rainbow, Gay Pride and why the Parade? I'm not opposed to any of the symbols and I could have Googled it, but I wanted my own understanding, something that me, myself and I could relate to.

I wondered about the Rainbow because a few months ago, I saw a post on FaceBook, an image of a pretty rainbow with the words printed above it **"A promise of God, not a symbol of Pride."** Along with a negative comment from the person who posted it. The tone of judgment annoyed me enough that I hid it from my feed but I kept thinking about it through the night and even into the next morning.

Finally I prayed about it, "Lord why is this bothering me?" and I looked up the story in Genesis 9:12 God said, "This (Rainbow) is the sign of the covenant I am making between me and you and every living creature with you, a covenant for all generations to come".

God creates the rainbow as a reminder of the promise never to flood the earth again. Great story. I read it a million times in VBS and knew it well but something caught my attention this time as I read it with the FB post in mind. My focus immediately went to the fact that God gave this promise to everyone for all time. It was then that I realized what was bothering me about that FB post. In my cynical state of mind the post implied (to me), that the rainbow was not a promise for everyone or at least not to the gay community. God's promise with the rainbow is for everyone. The work of the rainbow is done and when we see it, it should remind us that no one can stop it or remove it. The rainbow covers us all. The rainbow points to and gives me a beautiful picture of Jesus Christ, the promise of salvation and a reminder of God's love for each one of us. Again, no one can stop it or remove it. ….and it gets better… Later that evening I was reading a book titled THE CHILDREN ARE FREE (Re-examining the Biblical evidence on same-sex relationships) and came to the end of the book and on the very last page the author wrote: **"See you in heaven—let's meet beneath the rainbow that stretches over the throne of God.** (Rev 4:1-3)

Personally, I think the rainbow is the perfect symbol for the gay community.

Now, what about that pride? I was curious, why the emphasis on PRIDE as in, Gay Pride and the Pride Parade? I have this weird word association going on in my head with the word PRIDE. I thought being prideful was the same as being arrogant; some in the church might say that to be full of pride is to have a haughty spirit and no one would want one of those. My answer came on the day of the Pride Parade. Kathy was planning to go to the parade with us, so we were on the phone working out some details about who would drive, what time to go and where to park. (She had no idea I was praying for understanding.) She said "I want to stand in support of my friends and show respect to a community of people who have been forced to live in hiding and put to shame for too long. They don't have to be ashamed anymore." ... I said, 'Amen' to that. Her words gave me all I needed to understand and appreciate Gay Pride, and the Pride Parade.

Kathy picked us up and we were lucky to find a good parking spot only a few blocks away from 39th Street. We started making our way through a neighborhood street completely lined with cars and lots of people walking towards the parade. On our way we saw an old woman standing on her front porch, she was yelling at a young man, "I don't want your car in front of my house! You can't park here! I'll have your car towed!" And the young man hollered back, "Yes Ma'am, I'm movin' it!"

Then Kathy piped up with her *'that's not how this works, that's not how any of this works!'* voice, "ah-excuse me, (addressing the old woman). This street (pointing to the street), it's public property. You don't own the street" Then she turned to the kid and said. "You don't have to move your car. She doesn't *own* the street." (Then back to the old woman), "You don't own the street." (Then to the passersby), "the street *is* public property. He doesn't have to move." The old woman went inside, the kid moved his car and we kept walking.

I told you all that because it was kinda funny to watch, and I was impressed with the way Kathy stood up for the young man and wasn't rude or demanding to the old woman. She was just stating the facts. I thought it made a good picture of the attitudes towards the gay community. Maybe I am reading too much into this situation but remember, I prayed to see the spiritual texture in this day so stay with me. Let's say that the old woman represents ignorance and intolerance, the young man represents the gay community and in the middle is Kathy the ...mediator. It's people like Kathy that help bridge the gap between attitudes of ignorance and intolerance and the gay community. And even though the kid ended up moving his car, Kathy's attitude of mediator set a good example to anyone watching, namely me. I could not imagine being here without her.

Now on to the parade....

We made it to 39th street and met up with Parker, Kohl and about eight or ten of their friends. I stood there with Rex, Kathy and the boys taking it all in, looking around at the sea of people. I heard a buzz above our heads and saw a drone hovering at the corner of NW 39th and Penn. First time I ever saw one, but I knew what it was just as soon as I saw it. It surveyed the crowd as if to bare witness that I was there on this day, standing with my husband and son and a thousand more.

I was looking for some sort of sign or revelation whereas at one time in my life I feared the wrath of God in the form of a lightning bolt. It's true. About twelve years ago Rex and I accepted our first invitation to Michael and Richards Halloween party. Michael and Richard are a couple and they live at the end of our block in a great two story house. As Rex and I stepped off our door step and made our way to theirs, I swear for a split second, the thought crossed my mind that the Lord *might* strike us dead in our steps. Think about it, I was a "good Christian" woman celebrating Halloween with Homosexuals! Well, we made it home alive that day and my-oh-my how my thinking has changed. Richard and Michael have been nothing but good to us and we are so thankful to be neighbors. Oh, and guess what? I'm still a good Christian woman.

Back to the parade…

Several Businesses and Real-estate Companies showed their support and I now know what the 'Flying Spaghetti Monster" is, and that bummed me out until I saw not one, but two churches who support and welcome the gay community marching close behind. I miss church life sometimes. I miss praying with people and communion. I wondered if many people here at the parade go to one of those churches. At least they wouldn't have to worry about any gay bombs going off.

I am learning to settle down and not take offense or get upset every time I hear a negative comment or judgment against the gay community especially from the church. oh, it still stings, but now I can at least *try* to have a respectful conversation about it. In fact, I recently met with the pastor of then Crestwood Baptist, now Crestwood Vineyard Church. I wanted to meet with him because I was curious about what counsel he would have given us, if we had gone to him when Parker came out. He asked me if I wanted his answers from five years ago or from today. Of course I said, "Both."

He started with saying that five years ago he wasn't sure how he felt about women in ministry. Today he believes that the Holy Spirit works powerfully through women in leadership. Five years ago he had yet to counsel anyone with same-sex attraction whereas today he is ministering three individuals in his congregation. Five years ago he would have said, "Love the sinner, hate the sin." Today he would not. Five years ago, he would have referred us to the Baptist General Convention and they would have referred us to reparative therapy. Today he would not.

Today he hopes that the Church is a place where all feel welcome and that the Holy Spirit would be allowed to move freely and the love of Jesus would bring change in the lives of the people here.

I asked him if the church would allow a gay person to work with the youth or in the day care. He said that anyone who feels 'called to serve' should be allowed to serve in all areas of the church. On the subject of same sex marriage, he admitted that he personally was not ready to perform same sex marriages but there are others in authority within the

Vineyard church having discussions about it, should the law be passed. He went on to say that the church has a series of teachings they call, "Second Saturday" where an afternoon is spent on specific topics and they are working out the details on the issue of homosexuality. That it would be a time set aside for dialogue not a debate. We exchanged books that we recently finished reading on the subject and I was thankful for and encouraged by the conversation. Lastly, he apologized that the church family of five years ago was not able to be the comfort we needed.

I hope that he will remember our conversation and be sensitive to any person or family going through what we did, and I'm not saying I'm ready to sit in a pew, but I think it's important if someone like me could represent or at least try to be an advocate for the gay community in the more conservative churches. Not to scream and shout or protest out front, but to be that person in the church who could walk alongside the gay and the straight and the grumpy and simply pour into them love, hope and the promise of heaven. Today I pray that this church would be one that not only welcomes the gay community but could also send a message that you can be gay and Christian. Truth is, I don't know if this will be a message from Crestwood or at least not in my life time, but I do think the children of today's gay community could bring this message loud and clear if they hear it, but then again, how can they hear it if nobody say's it.

Oh my gosh....where was I.

The crowd rallied at the sight of two middle aged men waving from the sunroof of a big black Limousine. On the windows, written in white shoe polish, were the words: TOGETHER 21 YEARS AND STILL SHACKING UP! I thought it was a clever way to give a sarcastic nod to the ban against same sex marriage.

Next came a group of young people, some walking with hand-held signs and others marched together carrying a big colorful banner that read, 'BORN THIS WAY'. Oddly enough, when I saw the signs I thought of Westboro Baptist Church and a conversation I had with a new friend a few months ago.

Jim M. and I met through mutual friends and he offered to review and critique the first few chapters of this book, so I sent him what I had and a few days later we met for coffee and went over the story line. I was really impressed that he took such an interest with this story and by his comments I could tell that he spent some time going over each page. Finally he asked me if I considered adding anything about Westboro Baptist church. I paused for a moment and said, "I never thought about it" and I could tell by his expression that he was confused by my answer. I went on to explain that Parker was young at the onset of the Westboro conflict(s) and at the time of our meeting the founder of Westboro, Fred Phelps had just died. So really I just didn't concern myself with the issue. Besides, I don't agree with any of the teachings or practices of Westboro and the conflicts always seemed far away. I'm embarrassed to say I had the mentality of, 'Hey, as long as they ain't in my front yard...'"

Wait for it......Awkward moment about to become even more awkward.

Then Jim shared his story with me. He began with the fact that both he and his older brother Randy grew up gay in a small town. (Yes, you read it right, two boys, one family, both gay.) They grew up gay in the small town of Topeka, Kansas and they lived in a house that was located very near to (yep, you guessed it), Westboro Baptist Church. His family never went to Westboro Baptist but his mother was a very active member of a non-denominational church and she spent a lot of time trying to hide the fact that both of her children were gay. Her concern for the souls and wellbeing of her two boys, and the reputation of the family made for a stressful home life, not to mention the constant protests and media surrounding Westboro Baptist Church just blocks away.

Jim says life was especially hard for his older brother Randy who was 'never in the closet'. After Randy graduated high school he went to live with his uncle in Kansas City. The uncle began to suspect Randy of being gay and he set up one of his workers to come onto him, to see if he would take the bait. He did and the worker beat the holy hell out of him. When he returned home that night, all of his belongings were out on the lawn and he was told to leave and never return. Randy disappeared for months before calling his parents for help. He returned home, broken from living on the streets of California. After pulling himself together, he built himself back up. He eventually opened a gay bar called, "OZ" in Kansas. Initially his parents were embarrassed and distraught about it; an embarrassment to have something so unacceptable associated with the family. After a while the bar closed. He had a steady boyfriend that was accepted into his family. They would come over weekly, play games and have dinner together. He turned to selling Rainbow vacuum cleaners. Life was still a struggle and he decided to join the marines. When the AIDS crisis hit in the 80's and so many marines were being infected and not receiving any treatment or support from the military, he developed and managed a program to help them get benefits and medical attention. He had a longtime partner, a navy man. In the early 90's his partner died from complications of AIDS. Randy moved home, back to Kansas. He was reunited with his family and was soon stricken with AIDS himself. His parents took an early retirement and provided round the clock care for him, sometimes in their home and sometimes in the VA in Kansas, who hadn't had much experience with AIDS patients.

Suddenly the few chapters of my life that laid on the table before us, with the pages that Jim thoughtfully redlined and carefully highlighted, seemed so trivial. I sat there feeling shallow in light of his life, such a tragic and heroic story.

Jim went on to say that the Westboro Baptist Church controversy and the extreme efforts of Fred Phelps to turn the eyes of the world against the gay community has moved people to at least talk about the issue of same-sex attraction and then take a stand on one side or the other. Fred Phelps would be rolling over in his grave if he knew he has stirred a generation to stand in love and in favor of the gay community. His story stayed with me. I was touched by the bravery and struggle in the life of his brother. I saw myself in the thoughts and actions of his mother and the idea that any child would witness Westboro's hateful protests broke my heart. I was ashamed that I said, "I didn't think about it." I should have thought about it! I prayed about it, and was reminded of the holocaust and wondered if people who were so far removed or sheltered from such atrocities would have said the same thing! (Forgive me, I know this is a huge stretch in severity, mass genocide hardly compares to hateful protests at funerals but this is how my brain works people!)

Oh wow...back. to. the. parade.

Still standing at the corner of 39th and Penn the parade was winding down, surprisingly nothing too elaborate as far as floats go. Don't take this the wrong way, but I was expecting to see at least one grand and colorful float. There were two that were small in design. The effort was definitely there but hardly memorable. I saw beautiful drag queens dressed up and crowned like Miss America and Entertainers from a popular restaurant and bar called 'The Boom' and several groups marching from various clubs. Some couples rode in Jeeps and threw candy. A group of fifteen or twenty women all dressed in black carried a banner that read, 'Lesbian Mafia'. I don't know what kind of club that is? But I thought it was funny and decided that it really was no different than a group of straight men marching for Chippendales or calendar firefighters.

I looked around the crowd and saw such a diverse group of all ages. It really is amazing to me how many people are gay, not just here at the Parade, silly. I mean to say, that once you are aware of something, you see it everywhere.

For example, the last time I went to Target I saw three people I knew and they all just happen to be gay, now, it's true, I can be a social butterfly but what are the chances of seeing three friends or acquaintances (not together), at Target. Not to mention, two of those three don't live around here. Add to that number *at least* four people have come out as gay, lesbian and transgender, *all* of which were linked to Crestwood at one time or another during my time there. (I didn't see any of them at the parade.)

I wondered if my young friend Fernando was here. Fernando and I met through Jim M. on FaceBook. Jim M. was helping Fernando after he had been kicked out of his home and excommunicated from his church for being gay. When I first heard his story I immediately reached out to him and my heart was broken for him and his mother. I tried to encourage Fernando that his mother just needed time, and that she'll come around. It's been seven months and still no contact, except from the church elders. Apparently they required a meeting with Fernando demanding a confession so they could officially remove him from the church's membership. When he refused to meet with them, they went to his work and started harassing him until some co-workers intervened. I can't imagine how upsetting that must have been for Fernando. More than that I can't understand how a mother can stay away from her child.

Sometimes Fernando will posts poems on his FaceBook feed that are haunting; they give a glimpse of his heartbreak from the separation of family and friends.

> *Do you miss me sweet baby boy?*
>
> *Do you still call me uncle Nando?*
>
> *Have you forgotten about me?*
>
> *Remember my name?*
>
> *Do you complete sentences?*
>
> *Do you remember the sign language I taught you?*
>
> *Do you still love your ketchup?*
>
> *Still go to the house every Friday?*
>
> *Know that I love you more than anything…*
>
> *and miss you the most, baby boy.*

One Friday evening, Rex and I were walking home from "The Plaza," and we saw Fernando unexpectedly. He greeted me with THE best hug I have ever had. I mean he engulfed me, both arms embraced me so that my face was planted into his chest. I could have melted right into him. It was one of the most endearing hugs I have ever had. I'd go on to say that it was healing for both of us, and so memorable, that I'm still talking about it. Everybody should hug like that!

Focus Sara...the parade!

The evening sun was so bright that it made silhouettes on the sidewalk of Rex standing beside Parker. The image made my eyes water as I thought about all the years Rex stood by Parker when I couldn't, or worse, wouldn't. I can't imagine Parker's life without the continued support and unconditional love from his father. I am so thankful. If I could go back in time I would hug Parker tight on that first night that he came to me. I would tell him that he was brave and that God loved him no matter what anybody else said about him. I would have saved the journals from his youth, lost memories that were thrown away out of shame or from the complete lack of any personal privacy (you can thank me for that). I was blind to the opportunities to stand by and celebrate Parker and I'm sorry for casting shadows of doubt on the milestones of his youth. I regret freaking out and I fear that my reaction had an effect on Travis. I am afraid any resentment he might have towards Parker is because he saw how much it hurt me in the beginning. Hopefully he can see past all that, and treat it like a sickness that we are completely healed from now.

If I could go back in time I would educate myself on the subject of homosexuality when Parker first came to us and I would have been the first to start a dialog in my church about it with the people who knew us and loved us, even with the old people in the prayer circle. I'm not saying the discussion would have been received – but it would have been a start and talking about it is the first step to understanding. I would have stayed with my young friend in the kickboxing class and maybe we could have helped each other and I know for a fact that I'd be havin' a conversation with the instructor about *those* gates and these people...and I'd be about 10 pounds lighter. *KIA!*

Parade, Parade, Parade. geeze.

When the last of the parade marched by, the crowd started to mingle and gather in the center of the street. I remembered my prayers from earlier in the day and felt good about my understanding of the symbols that represent the gay community or at least what they now mean to me personally. As far as my prayer for the direction of this final chapter, definitely gonna be about the people I've met and the relationships made. Suddenly a memory from five years ago popped in my head.

I'm sitting at a Mexican Restaurant having lunch with a friend from church. All I can remember from the lunch is ...that goblet frosty beer drink with the lime and salt! Oh my gosh! Just kidding...all I can remember from that lunch is that my friend prayed over me (from across the table) that I would represent Jesus to the gay community, and that through me He would have such an impact on these people that they would be called out of this lifestyle and be forever changed. During that prayer I tried to conjure up images of me in a bible study or prayer time with *these* people. *Waaaoooowa.* The sincerity of that prayer *then* seemed so arrogant *now* and that memory literally took my breath away as I realized what we were asking and I fought to contain my tears and breathe through the brick-sized lump in my throat as I turned my face to the heavens and silently screamed from the top of my lungs, "THANK YOU LORD THAT I AM THE ONE CHANGED!"

I gathered myself enough to reconnect with the group standing around me. Rex by my side, Parker, Kohl and Kathy nearby and hundreds more gathered together – people of all ages and race, families with friends and couples standing together with no real separation or space between them. I noticed lots of people were waving rainbow colored flags or standing under rainbow colored umbrellas and the rainbow banners held high, even a lady standing in front of me had rainbow braids in her hair. I wondered if God were to look down from the heavens right then and there, and see all these colors, would it remind Him of His promise to us. I smiled as I thought that it would. It felt good to be here.

Satisfied with the time spent, like I had just finished a good meal and now it was time to head home. We started saying our goodbyes and I looked around at the crowd and bid a silent farewell and a feeling of camaraderie overcame me, it was a familiar feeling from times of fellowship at the church. My eyes focused on the big blue letters of the GOODWILL sign on the building across the street and I thought about Christmas and Jesus and the angels declaring "GLORY TO GOD IN THE HIGHEST, AND ON EARTH PEACE, AND GOOD WILL TOWARDS MEN." As I considered these things in light of my prayer to 'see' the Lord here, my thoughts were interrupted by a young black girl, maybe twelve or thirteen years old. She was walking towards me like she was on a mission, wearing a bright orange tank top and suddenly, like the drone, I knew it when I saw it! It was my confirmation, my perfect picture of the Lord's favor right here, right now in the form of this beautiful girl wearing a bright orange tank top with five simple words printed in bold letters: YOU CAN SIT BY ME.

WIDE EYED

Wide eyed at a starry sky
Star-shine golden falling down
I say to myself - oh to be a star
Oh - to be a star shining
Oh - to be a star shining in your eyes
Wide eyed at a starry sky
Star-shine brings angels to my mind
I say to myself - oh to be an angel
Oh - to be an angel singing
Oh - to be an angel singing hallelujah
Wide eyed at a starry sky
Star-shine brings love into my life
I say to myself - oh to be beautiful
Oh - to be so lovely
Oh - to be wonderful
Just like you are.

Words & music by Sara Cunningham, performed by Parker Cunningham

http://www.theburnfieldcastle.com/10_wide_eyed.m4a

CHAPTER NINE
BITS AND PIECES

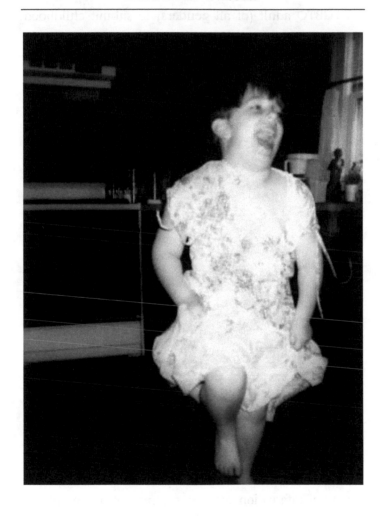

Parker submitted the following on March 2011 to the Born this way blog. A photo/essay project for LGBTQ adult (of all genders) to submit childhood pictures and stories reflecting the memories and early beginnings of the innate selves. Reprinted by permission from BornThisWayBlog.com

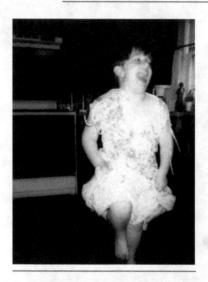

Nothing was more exhilarating than whirling and twirling in my mother's dresses. Here, I am wearing my favorite of hers. It was lightweight, covered in beautiful roses, and just sheer enough to feed my need to walk on the wild side. How my mother was surprised when my infatuation with boys came out in the open, I haven't the slightest idea. I think a lot of people that have struggled with being different wish their family would have walked them through the awkward glances, and the general lack of comfort that comes with growing up that way. Even so, I could never blame my family for being just as confused as I was, at the time. I remember feeling a little fancier than other boys my age. My concerns, were different from their concerns: Why would my cousin let her dolls have such ratty hair? If I couldn't have a purse, where was I supposed to put my things? Why didn't the Pink and the Red Power Rangers ever get together? I mean, they were both hot. It made sense. My VHS copy of "The Wizard of Oz" played a key role in my youth. The concept of some small town, decently pretty kid, being swept off to a faraway land - only to be truly wanted, occasionally envied, befriended by eccentrics, and come home at the end of the day having learned all of life's lessons - was the most perfect scenario I'd ever heard of. Pop culture was my first addiction, though. Late at night, in music videos, I'd catch glimpses of myself in people who seemed unimaginably confident and beautiful. That's all I've ever wanted to be. Since those days of twirling and brushing doll hair, I've found my beauty and comfort in creativity. I'm a stylist at the most rock 'n roll hair salon in Oklahoma. I'm also a musician, I'm an artist, I'm still fancy, and I'm still learning. I'm learning that it does get better. Exceptionally better.

Parker's first, famous-person same sex crush: Fred Savage (in "The Wonder Years")

The following is a letter I wrote to Parker. It was part of a "November Notes" project. (Basically, you send a note to someone every day for the month of November, but not to the same person ...and not the same note, silly)

Dear Parker,   November 1, 2013

I love you and wanted to take some time to share with you a few thoughts that I treasure in my heart about you.

On Monday nights we drive home on a route that takes us through the intersection of Classen and the NW Expressway. Every time we pass that intersection I telepathically send a message to your dad to turn left and then right to go to your street to do a 'drive by' of your house in hopes that you'll be on your porch and we can stop for a visit. Sometimes he gets the message and sometimes he doesn't.

I miss your clutter, sometimes.

Remember to have your oil changed.

Never stop singing and creating your art. It's all so beautiful and the world needs it. I am always so impressed with your many talents. You should come sing me a song right now.

If I could change one thing about our past, it would be our lives during your high school years. I would spend more time figuring who you are and what you were going through with you.

I love Kohl, I fell in love with him on our first visit in the back yard during the "20 questions" (as he puts it), when I saw the scars on his arms and heard the stories of his loss my heart loved him right then and there. Encourage him and build him up, he wants to take care of you, help him to do that.

I am so happy that we went to India together! That really was a trip of a life time that I will <u>always</u> treasure. I still can't believe it! The planes and trains and the hotel and the banner and the ocean! Oh my goodness, such a wonderful time. Remember how I cried when it was time to go? So embarrassing!

I love the fact that you recognize and embrace your own spirituality, your personal journey. Try to hold on to the good things that came from church life, not the lessons deemed out of ignorance or intolerance, but hold tight to the lessons of love, grace and mercy. I never met a person without a problem or a worry. Remember that everyone needs forgiveness and acceptance. Learn the difference between conviction and condemnation. Keep the Lord close, enjoy Him and love Him as He adores you. His goodness is everywhere and in every living thing. Look for it.

I love you so much.

Mom.

Travis:

Parker:

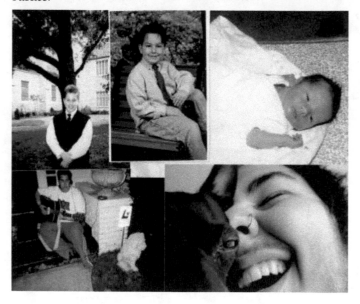

POTENTIAL PALACE
Little imagination and could be a dream

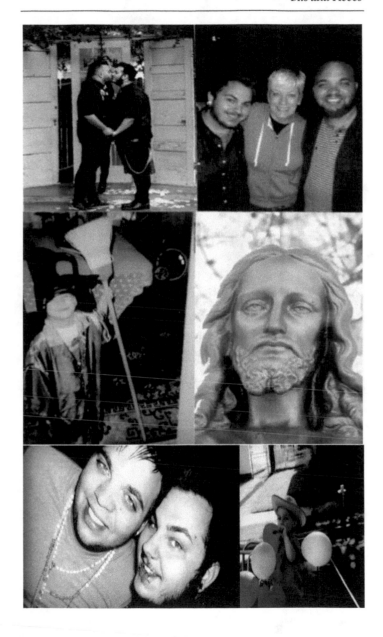

Daily Cow. You're Welcome.

•Songs: For the purpose of this book, two songs were recorded and the rest mastered by Ernie Tullis of PDM Recording Studio in Oklahoma City. **•Citations:** Chapter 7: All bible verses are from the New American Standard Bible. Geneses 5 outline adapted by El Shaddai Ministries Pastor Mark Blitz. Pictures of Grace adapted from Courson. J (2005) Jon Courson's Application Commentary. Volume 1. Nashville, Tennessee: Thomas Nelson. **•Photos:** Revel 8 Photo provided by: Todd Scott/ Wedding by: Chris Gann of Starving Dog and Nigel Bland of GOLDSTARLABS/ Parker with black guitar: Kohl w/Vibe (F)oto. / Kohl DJ: Michael Potts w/ Static X.

CPSIA information can be obtained
at www.ICGtesting.com
Printed in the USA
LVHW050258261021
701537LV00014B/678